**DISCARD**

# Riding

by **Dana Meachen Rau**

Reading Consultant: Nanci R. Vargus, Ed. D.

Marshall Cavendish
Benchmark
New York

# Picture Words

 bike

 camel

 elephant

 feet

 horse

 merry-go-round

 saddle

 seat

 sled

 ticket

 tracks

 train

 wagon

There are many things to ride.

Take a 🪑 and let's go!

A family rides in a .

The  moves on .

A boy rides in a 🛒.

He needs a friend to pull him.

A girl rides on her 🚲.

Her 👟 go up and down.

Kids ride on a 🛷.

They race down the hill.

A woman rides on a .

She sits in a 🏇.

A man rides on a 🐪 .

He sits on the hump.

A man rides on an .

He sits on its back.

Buy a .

You can ride on the  .

20

## Words to Know

**friend** (frend)
a person who you like to spend time with

**hill** a small mound

**race** (rayss)
to try to get to the end first

# Find Out More

## Books

Hubbell, Patricia. *Trains: Steaming! Pulling! Huffing!* Tarrytown, NY: Marshall Cavendish, 2005.

Hughes, Morgan. *Bicycles*. Vero Beach, FL: Rourke Publishing, 2004.

Ripple, William John. *Camels*. Mankato, MN: Pebble Books, 2005.

Walker, Pamela. *Train Rides*. Danbury, CT: Children's Press, 2000.

## Videos

Cornell, Jon. *Trains, Lots of Trains*. Meritage.

*I Love Horses!* Good Times Home Video.

## Web Sites

**Horses 4 Kids**
http://horses4kids.com/

**Kids Health: Bike Safety**
http://kidshealth.org/kid/watch/out/bike_safety.html

**National Railroad Museum**
http://www.nationalrrmuseum.org/

## About the Author

Dana Meachen Rau is an author, editor, and illustrator. A graduate of Trinity College in Hartford, Connecticut, she has written more than one hundred books for children, including nonfiction, biographies, early readers, and historical fiction. She likes to ride roller coasters with her family near her home in Burlington, Connecticut.

## About the Reading Consultant

Nanci R. Vargus, Ed.D, wants all children to enjoy reading. She used to teach first grade. Now she works at the University of Indianapolis. Nanci helps young people become teachers. She once rode an elephant through jungles in Thailand.

Marshall Cavendish Benchmark
99 White Plains Road
Tarrytown, NY 10591-9001
www.marshallcavendish.us

Copyright © 2007 by Marshall Cavendish Corporation
All rights reserved.
No part of this book may be reproduced in any form without written consent of the publisher.

All Internet sites were correct at the time of printing.

Library of Congress Cataloging-in-Publication Data

Rau, Dana Meachen, 1971–
Riding / By Dana Meachen Rau
      p. cm. — (Benchmark Rebus)
Summary: Simple text with rebuses explores various objects to ride, such as a camel, a sled, and a train.
Includes bibliographical references.
ISBN-13: 978-0-7614-2317-1
ISBN-10: 0-7614-2317-6
Rebuses. [1. Transportation—Fiction. 2. Rebuses.] I. Title. II. Series.

Editor: Christine Florie
Editorial Director: Michelle Bisson
Art Director: Anahid Hamparian
Series Designer: Virginia Pope

Photo research by Connie Gardner

Rebus images, with the exception of feet, provided courtesy of *Dorling Kindersley*.

Cover photo by Kwame Zikomo/*Super Stock*

The photographs in this book are used with permission and through the courtesy of:
*geogphotos/Alamy*: p. 2 (feet); *Photo Researchers*: p. 5 Lawrence Migdale; *Corbis*: p. 7 Jean Heguy; p. 13 Ariel Skelley; p. 21 Royalty Free; *Alamy*: p. 9 Kevin Brofsky; PhotoEdit: p. 11 Myrleen Ferguson Cate; *Getty*: p. 15 Photodisc Red; *SuperStock*: p. 17; *Index Stock Imagery*: p. 19 Dan Gair Photographic.

Printed in Malaysia
1 3 5 6 4 2